THE SECRET OF SELLING AND MOTIVATION

S=(P*ER)

Juan Pablo Alviar Malabet

THE SECRET OF SELLING AND MOTIVATION
S=(P*ER)
© Juan Pablo Alviar Malabet

Edited by: Corporación Ígneo, S.A.C.
For its editorial seal Ediquid
Av. Arequipa 185 1380, Urb. Santa Beatriz. Lima, Perú
First edition, November 2021

ISBN: 978-612-5042-48-4
Print on demand

Legal Deposit in Biblioteca Nacional del Perú N° 2021-13772
Impression finished in November 2021 at:
ALEPH IMPRESIONES SRL
Jr. Risso 580 Lince, Lima

www.grupoigneo.com
Email: contacto@grupoigneo.com
Facebook: Grupo Ígneo | Twitter: @editorialigneo | Instagram: @grupoigneo

Cover design: Mariana Barrientos
Translation: Alicia Mastrodomenico

Colection: Pensamiento

Content

DEDICATION

The book *The Secret of Selling and Motivation* is offered primarily to my family: my wife María del Valle and my children Bettina, Leonor, Isabella, Alexandra, and Jean, who have known how to live with me during my long trips. It's unconditional love that let us have a home.

I also dedicate it to my family, both those alive and who have already left, to my lifelong partners, employees, colleagues, and dear friends who have motivated me to write my first book, especially: Alfredo Vásquez, my brother Mingo and Alberto Rosales for their suggestions.

With all due respect, I also dedicate it to you, with the hope that this book will be of use to you, that in good times it'll be wonderful and that in difficult times you won't forget *The Secret of Selling and Motivation*, which will make the storm pass without a problem.

I also thank the different authors who accompany me in this book.

I thank the Pixabay portal (www.pixabay.com) for the beautiful images accompanying this work, made by talented photographers. As well as www.depositphotos.com.

And, of course, **to God**…

ACKNOWLEDGMENTS

Alfredo Vásquez, CEO and creative director of *Bodega Creativa*

As an advertising and marketing expert, I've always been passionate about the world of sales, especially strategies and the critical thinking behind them. I think that J.P. Alviar has managed to merge his experience and business knowledge with a very personal and close style in a brilliant way, making this book an accessible, inspiring, and clever way to comprehend and perfect the art of selling. Without a doubt, The secret of selling already is part of my professional consultation top.

Alberto J. Rosales R., lawyer, college professor, and article writer

Even though some people say that a good salesperson is born, Juan Pablo Alviar, an excellent friend, and seller, has proven this isn't the case and has managed to capture his business experience in Venezuela, Peru, and Colombia in a pleasant and easy-to-understand book for those who wish to develop or perfect their abilities as a salesperson. His teachings can be used for the development of other facets of life.

Alexa Rodríguez de Alviar, MSc and PhD in Educative Science

As a teacher in a permanent academic revision and facing the fact that I'm living in a country where it doesn't matter how much you strive to continue preparing yourself to improve your socioeconomic conditions, since it's evident that an educator's salary isn't enough, this work managed to inspire me.

The above situation led me to go to a person that is a motivator par excellence: a person capable of selling the unimaginable. After finding and receiving from him words of encouragement so necessary in times of crisis, he prompted me to enter the fascinating world of marketing as a complement to my teaching work. From that day, I verified that by dressing as *I want, I can*, and *I do*, you become a person capable of multiplying in hours and proportions of one to a hundred your monthly income. Forever grateful to J. P. Alviar. Thank you for teaching me the secret of selling.

Marialexandra Alviar, lawyer at *Sucre Energy Group*

It's a dynamic and innovative experience that connects with the reader from beginning to end and helps them strengthen their interpersonal abilities to position themselves as sellers in the digital era. In my personal and work experience in the energy area, *The Secret of Selling and Motivation* has given me the necessary tools to connect with elegance and creativity with clients, colleagues, family, and friends.

José Luis Gascue González, executive VP, is responsible for the worldwide sales of *Calinos Entertainment* in Turkey.

In my experience as a global content marketer, Juan Pablo Alviar's book, *The Secret of Selling and Motivation,* has caught my attention because it talks about universal sales techniques that can apply to any industry. It strikes me how this generality is applicable in different businesses; this might seem natural, but the analysis leads you to draw new conclusions and to observe new possibilities for productive business in any field, attesting that in the world of sales learning never ends.

I have known Juan Pablo since he was sixteen years old. He has always been a salesman who has known how to channel his skill, learn from his failures and successes, and turn his experience into innovative techniques that can be appreciated reading his book. I can only congratulate him for sharing his invaluable experience.

SYNOPSIS

It's an irrefutable truth that there is no company, no business, whether in the physical or digital world, without sales. With this clear, this book intends to share with you more than twenty-six years of activity and commercial experience, in which I discovered what is the secret of selling: Where is the secret of selling in times of crisis? and what is the secret of motivation? This knowledge and learning experience allowed me to solve the problem of selling and motivate in times of crisis.

That's what *The Secret of Selling and Motivation* is about, a book that surely will be very useful to everyone. I can affirm that the secret of selling works perfectly in regular times, in any country on this planet, and it has also been proven in times of crisis. After two experiences of my own, in two extreme scenarios: the economic and oil strike in Venezuela and now during the COVID-19 pandemic in Colombia and Peru, I can assure you that selling is possible in any scenario.

INTRODUCTION

More than forty years ago, when I was a young boy -about seven years old-, I discovered something I was very passionate about: Sales. One day, my mother needed money, and I told her, «I'll sell my toys!» And I did that. As a spoiled child, I had many toys, so many that I could sell some. In that experience, I discovered my passion for sales. I sold some of those toys to my little childhood friends, which they enjoyed very much, and the best of all was that I didn't part from them, as the friends that bought them were my playtime friends. So, this sale became an excellent business deal, and from it started my commercial history.

At a young age in my childhood, my father gave me a movie projector called Video 8. I remember that most of the movies were short films. At the time, I played the cinema and charged admission, and the payment might be candy. The best thing was that we all enjoyed and participated.

When I was twenty-two years old, my father gave me an amount of money with which I used to start my used vehicles import and export business, which was allowed during those times in Caracas, Venezuela, the city where I lived. However, I couldn't market those vehicles because they were too old. At that time, I was excited about entrepreneurship, but businesses don't always go well. I made a mistake bringing vehicles too old, and the issue became a problem, as I was about to lose the invested money, a quantity which would be important today.

However, I learned a lot from that experience. One of those lessons was that I discovered a business niche that didn't exist in Venezuela at the time, more than twenty-five years ago.

I refer to the programmed saving system or self-financing system, which was widely implemented in Brazilian culture. Group programming allows people to buy goods and services cheaper than through bank financing or cash purchase. This business consists of forming groups of natural or juridical persons who acquire goods or services without initial or interests. However, I won't talk about this venture, in which I have more than twenty-six years of activity and experience. This book intends to share how I discovered the secret of sale: Where is the secret of selling during times of crisis? And, what is the secret of motivation? Since this discovering allowed me to solve these problems during the «bad» times. I thus proceeded to move our sales force to obtain results and meet the commercial objectives. That is what this book is about, which surely will be most beneficial for everyone, to share all this knowledge simply and practically.

I can affirm that the secret of selling works perfectly in regular times, in any country on this planet still, I also have proven it, after two experiences of my own lived in two extreme scenarios, as the economic and oil strike in Venezuela and now during the COVID-19 pandemic in Colombia and Peru, that this secret works also in times of crisis. Also, I dare say that it works during war times, during an alien visit, or even in a zombie invasion, ha, ha, ha, may God protect us; what I'm trying to say with these extreme and surreal examples is that we sell to people and they always, in any scenario, find themselves in need to buy.

I was finishing high school, at eighteen, when my mother had an import-export business. She told me: «Son, we have one thousand wheelchairs, and we haven't been able to sell them,» to which I replied: «Don't worry, mom.» She told me: «We have made every effort to sell those wheelchairs and haven't been able to. We have the whole stock.» Then I offered myself: «I can sell them, but you'll have to pay me a commission.» I remember well this conversation with my beloved mother around 1988. With the desire and motivation to help, I planned how I would sell the wheelchairs. Luckily, I saw a fair of medical equipment import-export companies during Holy Week, so I prepared myself and approached them instead of going to the beach with my friends. I spoke to each person at the fair and managed to sell a thousand wheelchairs, which my dear mom had for over three years. It was then when I could truly comprehend that, to successfully sell, you need preparation, contacts, relationships, and propose a goal.

I was born into a family of professionals. My father was a civil engineer, as one of my brothers. My eldest brother is a doctor, and my mother is a merchant. During high school, I thought I was going to be a doctor. I had been accepted at college thanks to a national award for my student thesis. However, I was also interested in a law degree. On my last day, before graduation, I was asked: «What are you going to study?» I hadn't even told my friends or family, who were surprised when they heard, «Juan Pablo Alviar, a law student» during the graduation. Why did I make that decision at the time? For my passion for sales, for business. I saw my brother, the doctor, as an extremely good person, highly humanitarian, with a vocation of service and a passion for health, but I thought: «How does a merchant fit into medicine? If what I like is to sell.» I felt that blood running through my veins, the salesman's blood, so I told myself: «No, I'll go to law school!» as I saw it as a complement of my passion. I wasn't wrong. That is another subject I'm very passionate about, the law that today serves me as a tool, as it has allowed me to fill in positions as legal director.

I emphasize: I have the salesman and entrepreneur's blood as it can be seen in the experience I brought from Brazil and, although not all businesses succeed, from it arose the activity that I have been doing for many years, not only in Venezuela but in other Latin American countries as Colombia and Peru. I made three attempts before starting that activity, all of which failed until we finally made it work. Today I have the same business partners from twenty-four years ago, but that is another story.

After many years of experience, I have built a wealth of knowledge in the sales area that backs me today up to talk and advise on this topic, tell the commercial story of living sales and the journey, the situations I have seen, and the secret of selling, motivation, and retail passion that one can have in life. As a first principle, I can say that we're all sellers, but a salesperson must feel passionate about what he does. You must take on challenges and goals and learn to move, be dynamic, active, want to achieve, and do. If you're willing to do all these, welcome to this path; I hope it'll benefit you, my dear friends, because we're already friends.

Do you like and are passionate about commerce and business? Then, I invite you to know the secret of selling and motivation. I don't pretend this book to be a monologue. I want to write it together. With our experience, we'll build our commercial secret based on what we have learned in our field. We'll talk about the professional salesperson characteristics, the superhero or superheroine vocation, how to win customers, motivation and sales, announcing their respective secret, their mathematical formula, the process of selling, objections, how to increase our effectiveness, and in reflections.

To whom is this book for? To anyone who likes business, commerce, sales, being an entrepreneur; to any professional salesperson, any commercial director, consultant, manager, sales executive, and any person that wishes to know the secret of selling and motivation; to anyone who wants to learn how to be more effective, more efficient and, of course, how to obtain better results.

Remember that there is no company, no business, either physical or digital, without sales.

CHAPTER 1

CHARACTERISTICS OF A PROFESSIONAL SALESPERSON

A professional salesperson

Let us stop at this first topic of the book; let us talk about who is the salesperson, who is that person that occupies perhaps one of the most critical positions in a company. If there are no sales, dear friends, there is no company, whether your own or of a third party. It applies to any business: restaurants, services companies as insurance, car or motorcycles dealerships, banks, technology business, personal activities; all, no matter the field, require a sales force. For example, if you like someone, you must show your best way to win that person: sell yourself. Among the multiple definitions of what selling is that we can find on the Internet and many books about sales, we can see that selling is the art of being able to convince, the skill to create a relationship, value. In this sense, I can affirm that **we're all sellers**, consciously or unconsciously, we're continuously selling, through our image, our knowledge, when we apply for a job, when we offer a product, in short, we sell on several occasions.

Its origin comes from the Old English word *sellan*, «to sell,» which is the action and effect of selling (to give the property of something to another person after the payment of a stipulated price for the good or service). For example, «The bicycle sale was a success: we have received more money than expected; the sale was a conquer.» «Juan Pablo is a programmed saving system seller.»

Now, the main issue to deal with is the person. Who sells? How to sell? Who should it be? Whats is the salesperson's profile? Which should be the salesperson's characteristics, whether physical or virtual?

I, therefore, invite you to answer these questions. I have left some space for you to write which should be that salesperson's characteristics. How is that superman or superwoman who moves the business, believes in the economy, builds relationships, and makes money and experience? Tell me then, how should that person be? You have a lot of space to write those characteristics that identify a professional salesperson.

A professional salesperson is:

Interdependent

One of the characteristics of a professional salesperson is interdependence. What does it mean? What does interdependence mean? What does it mean to be dependent as a professional salesperson?

Without a doubt, a salesperson is a person that depends on others with which relationships are built to make commercial interchanges, as we don't sell to aliens, nor objects; we sell to people in this world. Therefore, an interdependent professional salesperson depends on the people, their relationships, and their whole environment.

Interdependence refers to the set of bilateral relationships established among persons. In this sense, interdependence is an equally dependent relationship in which all its participants are mutually beneficial, complementary or subsidiary in many ways.

This is also reflected in our lives. That circumstance in which we interact with others determines our positive or negative relationships with people. For example, an organization is nothing more than a group of interdependent individuals who perform different but complementary roles together that work toward a common goal.

Open

Another characteristic of a salesperson is openness. What does it mean? It means that they're a person open to change, without prejudices. In this context, people can freely communicate with the seller, either through a physical or digital channel, because they build confidence. It's a person that doesn't critic nor speak ill of others, conciliatory, attentive, polite, provides solutions, and pays attention.

Define what you think of an open person:

Are you open?

An open person is splendid, won't be quick to judge others, accepts differences in thought and culture, always willing to learn from others, is an available picture easy to change.

How to be more open to others? First, you must show yourself genuine, authentic, close to others. To be more open is necessary to develop communicational skills that allow you to interact efficiently when talking to others, have an open body language, ask questions freely, have mutual interest and an empathetic attitude, pleasant or welcoming.

Receptive

A professional salesperson is receptive; it means they listen, see, watch, and understand.

In the field of interpersonal relationships, the acceptance of people, the capacity to listen, weigh, recognize, and go along with other ways of thinking, act and living in a different way than their own allows them to get close to others. In this way, the value of receptivity points to a person's virtue in consenting to others' suggestions to improve one's own abilities.

Define with your own words a receptive person:

Are you receptive?

Draw what it means to be open and receptive:

High contact

Another characteristic is **high contact**. A professional salesperson is a person that creates and keeps many connections, that prospects. This means that he interacts with people through any physical means or email, calling, WhatsApp, social media, or any other existent way to communicate. A professional salesperson is a person who promotes high contacts, and these produce considerable benefits. There is always a win-win situation in this commercial exchange. The more connections, the more rewards will be obtained (contact factory). These interactions are necessary because the salesperson is responsible for bringing their business or companies to customers as first image. Hence, their focus is on establishing relationships with as many people as possible, using their own efforts, advertising, or market.

Analyze and give your opinion about building contacts:

Express your conclusions:

Well-informed

Another characteristic of a professional salesperson is to be **well-informed**.

What does well-informed mean to you?

At first, to be well-informed in the sales topic means to dominate totally and wholly the knowledge about the product or service offered. I must know its benefits or drawbacks and be informed about my environment, what is happening, and what happened, for example, with the COVID-19 pandemic. This way, they will have greater control over commercial relationships. It's important to remember that we're alive, that the world doesn't stop, that we all have needs and dreams to achieve.

Being well-informed means solving different situations and moments related to our good market research or environment. Experiences of others that have faced the same difficulties allow us to advance in our work. This way, the knowledge we have absorbed is transferred to other people involved in our same commercial activities.

Draw what it's like to be well-informed in the commercial world:

Plan their work

To plan means to organize. In this sense, planning the work means establishing the timeframes used in each activity, how it'll be done, and the steps to follow to achieve the proposed goals. It also means to have enough time to rest, the daily and familiar time, and recreational activities. Each thing requires its time. The most valuable thing we have in our actions is time, and we must optimize it.

Any plan is a systematic set of activities carried to realize an action. This way, the plan satisfies necessities or solves specific scenarios or situations.

From my point of view, time is the most valuable thing in life, since it's our time and we must manage it effectively to account for productive, educational, family, personal, sports, or recreational activities, to have a good successful life. The sum of time is the result of our life, which has a beginning and an end. The secret is to distribute and organize the time to meet each of our requirements. The work plan will be the route that will allow you to experience a full and productive life in each of its facets.

What do you think about this?

We're talking about the characteristics of a professional sales-person. This person is a superhero who manages their time, keeps planning, and can work wherever they are.

Sleep less

I'm sorry, but this is a personal consideration, and it's obviously optional for you. It means to me not to lose time sleeping. That time will come. Life is lived awake, not asleep.

What do you think about this?

Yes, there is time for everything, even to rest from a good job or responsibility achieved, to spend time with our loved ones, family, and friends.

I respect your opinions but, I insist, to me, life is lived awake. Make your time count!

The Bible tells us in some of its verses: «Redeeming the time» (Ephesians 5:16). «Redeeming the time, because the days are evil» (Colossians 4:5). «Walk in wisdom toward them that are without, redeeming the time» (Daniel 2:8). «The king answered and said, I know of certainty that ye would gain the time, because ye see the thing is gone from me.» (Psalms 90:12). «So teach us to number our days, that we may apply our hearts unto wisdom.»

Time must be seized. I have often heard couples saying, «How was your day at work?» to which is answered, «I had a tiring day, I worked a lot.» Suppose you objectively analyze what many people do during their day; you'll see that a lot of time has been misspent, distracted by other matters, as having conversations in the middle of the working day about sports, show business, soap operas... By this, I don't mean that it shouldn't be done, but we must know how to separate the working from the distraction time to control what I'm spending my time on. How much time do I work really?

Speak just enough

For me, a professional salesperson is a fair and balanced person, that doesn't exaggerate nor is overtly passionate. Their message and voice are weighted. Speak and says what is necessary.

What is your opinion about this?

Do you share this characteristic? Why yes, and why not?

Speak accurately

Everybody, some more than others, speaks and answers impulsively, without thinking about what is said. This causes problems in our lives and our business ventures. We must learn to express what is necessary and accurately, listening and answering what is asked and not something else.

We can't act according to action-reaction or speak impulsively, and it's fundamental to listen, process, and then answer what is asked precisely. We aren't robots; we're thinking and reflective beings.

We must apply this not only in selling but also in our social and familiar life. That way, we'll avoid pointless and draining problems.

Sell and advise

This fighting entrepreneur has two objectives: sell and advise. The intention is to create a lifelong relationship with their client and, of course, gain money through good work.

What does the dictionary tell us?

Sell: transitive, intransitive verb[1]
1. To give something to somebody in exchange for money. «He sold his vehicle to buy a house.»
2. To offer something for people to buy. «My father sells jewerly.»
3. To be bought by people in the way or in the numbers mentioned; to be offered at the price mentioned. «The book sold well and was reprinted many times.»

---

1   Oxford Learner's Dictionaries. (n.d.). Sell. In Oxfordlearnersdictionaries. com dictionary. Retrieved October 20, 2021, from https://www.oxford-learnersdictionaries.com/definition/english/sell_1

4.   To accept money or a reward from somebody for doing something that is against your principles. «He sold his accomplices to reduce his time.»

5.   To persuade somebody that something is a good idea, service, product, etc.; to persuade somebody that you are the right person for a job, position, etc. «You really have to sell yourself at a job interview.»

6.   To make people want to buy something. «It's quality not price that sells our products.»

A **salesperson doesn't do anything else but sell**; this is their reason for being. In the commercial world, this must be very clear. A seller isn't a promoter showing a product or service; they're made to close business deals and receive money for their professional or commercial work.

A professional salesperson advises, is a consultant, and recommends their product, service, or business because they believe in what they do. This is what makes them gain reputation and success.

What is a commercial adviser?

What is a business consultant or commercial adviser? What kind of message do they transmit? As it was previously said, a business consultant is a link between the client and the company. In the negotiations with a customer, a good business consultant must report the following in a truthful and timely manner: products and services characteristics, the benefits these products or services can give them, conditions of sale, forms of payment, delivery conditions, or provision of services, as to establish the after-sales channels and, of course, to attend their client continuously.

In the same way, a commercial adviser also communicates with their attitude and presence, beyond words or documents presented to the clients. A commercial adviser is the image of the company. Their attitude and presence will reinforce or nullify a potential client's idea about the company or brand.

In the pre-sale stage, the seller can obtain important information about the customer and the competition. That information won't only be helpful for him during the presentation, handling objections, and closing of the sale, but for the company's commercial and market strategies.

For this, the business or commercial adviser must fulfill their closing informant role, show effective communication, and have certain personal qualities and emotional intelligence to **satisfy** their future client.

How must be given the information by a sale or commercial adviser?

It must be assertive, proactive, transparent, timely, and truthful, for which the adviser must foresee possible questions and objections the client may present to act accordingly. The communication must be based on **knowledge**. If a commercial adviser doesn't know the product or service they offer, they won't adequately communicate its characteristics and benefits.

Provide a good service

They're committed to their relationships, others, the company, with whatever they may do. Therefore, pay attention to others' necessities and create a trustworthy environment. They're helpful and interested in people. They offer quality services to satisfy their customers; that is their primary goal. The client is the most important thing, and we're responsible for being the first image of our service and product. **The client is our boss.**

In this regard, allow me to bring this experience: once, I went to buy a car. A seller was reading a magazine while I was watching the car I wanted. Do you think the salesperson came, said hello or anything? Not a thing, I just left and never bought a car from that dealership.

Providing a good service or optimal customer service is fundamental when selling a product or service. People aren't only interested in those; they're also looking to be well served.

There is a word I like a lot: servuction. This is the process made inside of companies or businesses to offer a service to a customer.

Servuction is a neologism that defines the manufacturing process of services within the organization, which involves physical and human elements in the relationship with customers to provide the best service that satisfies their needs and demands. It sees the company as a system manufacturing service. This was proposed by the French professors Pierre Eiglier and Eric Langeard in their book *Servuction, le marketing des services*, published in 1987.

Therefore, your customer must perceive a good service or, instead, **the best service** through all their senses. We're responsible for our client perceiving it this way.

Examples of offering benefits

Customers benefits:

The cheapest way for people to finally decide buying a good or service they have dreamt of.

A service they need.

Everybody can achieve their dreams. Simple and accessible.

Creative

Being creative is about having innovative ideas, searching for alternative solutions. A creative person is attentive, watches their environment to create good things and to share them.

Starting from the premise that we're all creative, I recommend you read about creativity to better develop this skill. This capability is grown like the one of being an excellent professional seller or athlete.

If you have a new idea, whether for yourself, your business, or service, put it in motion. It just takes creative people to get ahead. Be creative.

Creative people have in common their enthusiasm, imagination, and, above all, confidence in themselves because they show something new they thought. We must live with inspiration. Let's find what inspires us.

Let me tell you that creating products and implementing new things are some of my best hobbies. About four years ago, I had the vision to transform my business venture into the digital world. It was a traditional business with more than forty-eight years in the market. I converted one of its commercial processes to digital. After studying the national and international competition in our line of business, I saw that none had a digital app as I had conceived it. I'm happy about it. I invite you to develop this new habit every day. If your company or activity isn't in the digital world, hurry up. Along the way, you'll find resistance, but step by step, everybody will see the importance of creating, innovating, and applying.

«I'm not creative» is the answer many people give.

Any idea is creative; we're all creative, we all have imagination. We mustn't forget that the steps that allowed us to obtain any product or service were those of creatives worldwide. To innovate is to apply creativity over specific situations, do make something more attractive and that it impacts.

One example of this is to improve a product, service, or process to meet commercial or market conditions. Among the improvements we can contemplate: making sure the users and clients are delighted with the product or service offered, meeting their expectations, increasing the brand's value, or decreasing costs.

We must manage innovation as one more area in our companies, assigning it a budget and applying techniques to generate creative ideas in each work session.

I spent time in this subject because I consider essential the creativity applied to business. A good executed idea gives good results. Good ideas must prevail; that is the best strategy in times of crisis for a professional salesperson, entrepreneur, merchant, or any person seeking a goal, whether personal, business, group, community, or social. The tricky thing is to implement a good idea.

What can you say about my affirmation?

Take the floor and define what it's to be creative in your activity:

Innovative

Another characteristic related to creativity is innovation. The Oxford Learner's Dictionary defines innovation as «introducing or using new ideas, ways of doing something.»

In this sense, a professional salesperson must be attentive to improve their person, products, or processes. This makes them innovative people. They'll be responsible for introducing products and services in the market considering the customer's needs.

Innovation is a change that implements novelties, which refers to modifying existing elements to improve them, even though it's also possible to implement new features. There is a form of innovation consisting in the improvement of business management with new procedures, in the use of technology, automation, perfecting quality, defining new ways to satisfy the customer. The above are only some of the benefits of innovation. I insist, innovation is a critical factor in the business development and economic growth of countries.

In economy, Joseph Schumpeter introduced this concept with the theory of innovations that appears in his work *The theory of economic development* (1934), in which he defines innovation as the establishment of a new function of production. Economy and society change when the production factors merge in a novel way. He suggests that inventions and innovations are the keys to economic growth. Those who usually implement those practical changes are the entrepreneurs. We also observe that those who invest the most in research and development achieve the most wealth.

Are you innovative?

Initiative

They have a lot of initiative. A professional seller is the one who takes the lead. They start early each day, take the first step, always try to be first while collaborating with friends, family, co-workers, and people. One of their main characteristics of having initiative is that it's born from everyone; that is, there is no external factor that drives them to achieve their goal. The initiative moves people on many occasions to make decisions on their own, without persuasion from others. The initiative is also the personal quality that usually generates projects, proposals, and solutions to problems we may face daily.

For you, what is taking the initiative?

Professional

A professional salesperson is someone who has prepared themselves over time, learned quickly, is well-informed, has developed abilities that others lack, is specialist in their field, knows details of the goods and services they offer, their benefits, disadvantages, and advantages. From my point of view, they don't need a professional degree, but they do need a lot of training since selling is one of the most demanding professions there is, because there is a goal to meet and have results. Companies of any kind exist thanks to sales, which is the first income of a business.

Obviously, thousands of self-taught people in the world have been successful without any degree, so beyond academic education, the most important thing is training. I recommend that we constantly study, and if we have courses or degrees, we'll be better prepared, with more life tools.

Therefore, if we decide to be sales professionals, we must be carriers of knowledge, specialization, and discipline. In short, I am a professional because I am, and I consider myself a professional.

What do you think about my statement?

Name successful sellers of their products and services who don't have college or technical degrees.

A professional is an expert in a task, a person whose life purpose is realized through the practice of a specific competitive activity. The term is also associated with preparation standards that allow the activity members to perform certain functions.

Professional salespersons earn from their service, which is «selling»

What is the name of the remuneration or fees that commercials receive for their service of selling?

Commissions, percentages, prizes, bonuses, remunerations, salaries, participation, premium, brokerage, retribution, part, gratification, fees, monthly payments, annuities, compensation, wage, fare, assignation, or credit. **Money**.

They do

They're made. A professional salesperson must know about the matter at hand, as an athlete who practices every day. They train, study, know new techniques daily, document themselves, and consistently seek to improve their practice in the commercial field or within their company or home.

Athletes and professional salespersons share some traits, as:

Passion or enthusiasm: they show love for what they do. It's the strength that keeps them working through the long hours, without weekends or vacations.

Steadfastness: when everything is perfect, it's easier to be a professional salesperson. But an actual professional salesperson keeps insisting even when things are complicated, and they usually refuse to accept failure in the pursuit of results (sales). The same strength a player in any sports team must have.

Self-confidence: a professional seller is more likely to make commitments just because they're convinced that they'll obtain good results with their capabilities. Same as in sports, where feeling competent is essential to achieve success.

Resistance to failure: a professional salesperson overcomes loss and keeps going, reinvents themselves, and prepares for the next activity to sell, same as an athlete that may lose a competition but is ready for the next one.

Explain, how an athlete is like a professional salesperson?

There are many companies worldwide that search for salespersons, but, in the topic at hand, you must know the characteristics to be a great professional and what companies are demanding their work teams so you can take into account:

- Knowledge.
- Experience.
- Positive and pleasant attitude.
- Relationship with people.
- Compromise.
- Initiative.
- Adaptation.
- Vocation.

These are some characteristics any professional must have to do a good job and be valued by others in the working field. One of the spaces where the term **experience** is more relevant in the workplace is that when companies start personnel selection processes, they bet, primarily, to hire the most experienced candidates in the area they need to cover. About this, there must be said: the practice and the experience are the most valued.

Benefits

They offer benefits. A professional salesperson shows the benefits the product or service provides to potential clients. They're committed to their brand, product, service, entrepreneurship, and environment. Believing in the product means transmitting and showing the advantages, benefits, and best conditions for their customers. **You must be a buyer of what you sell.**

Benefits that your clients expect from your product or service

In sales, there is always said that the value of a product or service must justify the price. Likewise, the work of a professional salesperson is to convince their prospects of the real value of the product or service.

The customers expect different benefits or advantages of the products or services offered and purchased, as: their functionality, that is, their usefulness; high satisfaction with the purchase, based on experience.

From these benefits, the most powerful is the customer experience on the purchased item. Therefore, it's there where most of our effort must be with our future clients since a satisfied client will generate more sales.

Customer experience management (CEM or CXM) is the practice responsible for understanding, designing, and managing the interactions with clients to influence their perceptions, significantly to increase their satisfaction, loyalty, and support to our brand, product, or service.

The human being can learn from experience. That knowledge is related to the proceeding and the empirical. The usefulness or value of the experience will depend on each person. The term experience refers to situations never experienced before and that are carried out to discover new pleasures or simply reveal new experiences that impact our perceptions of things.

Examples of experience

Appreciate the good taste of a meal, the wonderful aroma of perfume or coffee, share with family and loved ones, the treatment we receive: «It makes me feel very good.» **«What a lovely person.» «What a sublime product and service»**… The perception our client must experience is to feel they have a product and service different from everything that exists or has known before, that is, our product or service excites our customer in the best way.

They work

They work in the short, medium, and long term. A professional salesperson is a person who plans their work and does it in the short, medium, and long term. Therefore, they work to see results day by day and for the future. Hence the importance of organization, planning, and discipline. They have the whole set of characteristics mentioned in this section. Thus, every excellent salesperson knows that any hour, minute, and week are valuable, that they'll have to do the plan to obtain the expected results and achieve the objectives set. All these results are measurable. A professional salesperson **isn't weak nor tired**.

For you, what is working in the short, medium, and long term?

They're concerned

They worry about their client. They're sincerely interested in their client; they're restless and offer something perceived as good by themselves because they believe they have proved it or it serves them. They see the benefits and advantages, and as good people, they want to give this good news to their clients; that is why they care. But this means they aren't a person who buys others' problems; they don't carry them but help them.

I always say that I only carry my children in my life, which was only when they were little, but I help them and push them. What is sought with the client is to offer them solutions. I recommend that we find products and/or services that we would buy ourselves to start an entrepreneurship; this will give us great strength: believe in **what we sell** or do daily.

«Win-win» is a strategy popularized by Stephen Covey in his book *The 7 Habits of Highly Effective People* (1997). The process is that given two parties that reach an agreement, it's beneficial for both.

Always win

I share with you the life option that is to win consistently, and this doesn't mean that the other loses; the other must win the same as us, that is, it's an equitable relationship, but always winning is related to doing what we like the most, by doing this we're constantly winning. Therefore, I invite you to find in your life what are you passionate about, and if you can transform it into a business or link it to sales, all the better. I communicate that to consistently win is to do the most exciting thing for yourself in any activity we develop. Let's try to find in our life what we like the most. It isn't an easy task to achieve, but we'll lead a full and productive life by attaining it.

What kind of relations must you find in your life?

They develop

They develop their portfolio. They're interested every day in their client base and potential customers, called prospects. I must build, develop, and maintain my client portfolio. The hard work was already done, that was selling; now the easier starts: keep your customer and increase your sales with them while you're looking for new prospects.

Why is it essential to maintain and manage the client portfolio?

It's because in the lean times or low sales periods, or when the competition appears or becomes more substantial, the client portfolio is a crucial tool to expand the market and overcome difficulties or crises. The most important thing to form a portfolio is to define a client profile and the target market you want to reach. There are great sales opportunities in the current client base; the hard work is already done. This doesn't mean leaving behind the search for new customers; still, you must consider that it's always easier, quicker, and affordable to sell more services or products to existing customers.

It's essential that each customer generates new clients for you and that each of those generate two, three, or four new clients, which will start the exponential growth of your portfolio. Start by offering your product or service to your acquaintances and clients. The secret to maintaining and growing your customer base is called tracking. A client's loyalty can't be bought; it must be promoted through attention, constant and personal communication. A customer proud of the offered service will easily recommend it to others. The important thing is to have a lasting and reliable relationship with our client portfolio, which starts with the **quality of sales** made from the beginning. Consider your positive attitude as a fundamental principle of action; this marks the beginning of a permanent business relationship.

Recommendation: always perform an after-sales service, which consists of verifying that the customer is delighted with what was bought, whether product or service.

Among all the customers, they can identify which are the closest clients and the least. Make them comfortable, happy, and special. Today's most essential thing is attracting customers and knowing them, providing personalized service, considering their preferences, tastes, wishes, and necessities.

They're disciplined

They're disciplined. Being disciplined is a crucial habit to achieve success in everything we develop. From a very young age, I studied in a school and college that trained me, as my family, in what I am today. As for discipline, I was in a military band for seven years during my childhood and adolescence. From that time, I have kept lifelong friends that are practically my brothers (Héctor, Alfredo, José).

The precepts of the military band of the Saint Ignatius of Loyola school, which has more than seventy years of history, are: sacrifice, honor, and discipline. Being disciplined is a set of habits and rules that help us achieve our proposed goals. I would say that's one of the keys to success in our professional life. Discipline can be developed and built, but it isn't easy; it's achieved with effort and dedication.

Discipline is the ability some people must put into practice a series of principles related to order and perseverance, both in professional and personal aspects.

In this regard, discipline supposes the capacity to control impulses, especially those that keep us from achieving our goals and incline us to enjoy the most immediate charms. The earliest direction is given to children at home by their parents or persons in charge of their upbringing, and it's related to the establishment of a bedtime, meal hours, or personal hygiene habits, as other issues related to the behavior at home and outside it.

Later, the children receive school discipline, where they learn how to relate with their peers and teachers, fulfill their homework, and follow the rules; it means the code of conduct the school tries to enforce to ensure coexistence, order, and the functioning of the institution.

Also, the definition of discipline includes habits, rules, norms, and dispositions that must be followed by religious, military, company, or organization members to guarantee order, the efficient execution of activities, and the achievement of objectives, related to the institution which they belong.

Are you disciplined?

Are you consistent in what you do?

Discipline is developed by repeating many times tasks or activities until they become a part of us, we get used to them, and they become routine for us. For example, I never made my bed when I got up but, during the COVID-19 pandemic, I learned a new habit: make my bed when I get up. And now, it's part of my daily routine.

They're constant

Constancy isn't a very common virtue among people, and it's an excellent marker of differences. While it's true that dedication and constancy are necessaries to keep us active within a society, our job or entrepreneurship, it's no less accurate that humanity hasn't advanced through pre-established means, but through the breakdown of these in search of new horizons, that is, the world changes with every broken paradigm. Then, being constant implies facing a series of vicissitudes, difficulties, and problems, without being discouraged by those or taking away the desire to keep on going until achieving what has been proposed. It's a correct attitude, given that knowledge and skills are of little use without constant work, exposure, the richness of a lived and lasting experience over time.

From the Latin word *constantia*. Constancy is firmness and perseverance in resolutions. It's an attitude or mood predisposition towards a goal. So, steadiness is the **focus** we have to perform an activity and reach a wish that has to be fulfilled, so no difficulty or obstacle deviates from that course to achieve the goal or goals set. I can't go in life as a weathervane. I must decide on a route and follow that path; even if challenges arise, I must overcome them. If we fall, we'll rise again and clean the blow to continue. That's constancy, also a secret to success.

Let us be focused on our aspirations, my dear friends.

They're fighters

They're fighters. A person born to work and with their effort overcome obstacles, achieve goals and objectives. A fighter rises and is ready for the daily battles in their life; they aren't defeated. This is a samurai.

One of the principal characteristics of a fighter is that they don't surrender in front of life obstacles. They're people that, even if things go wrong, don't give up. Therefore, they're persistent and overcome difficulties that come their way. **They also know what they want and, because of that, don't rest until they get it. They face fear, overcome it and continue to persist until they reach.**

Inspiring quotation

There are men that fight one day and are good. Others fight one year and they're better. There are those who fight many years and are very good. But there are the ones who fight their whole lives, those are the indispensable ones.

Bertolt Brecht

Are we fighters?

The term fighter has equivalents in different countries. For example, the expression *berraco* in Colombia means a brave, enterprising person; *arrecho* in Venezuela is related to hard-working people. Obviously, we're aware that these words may have another meaning in each country.

Say what the popular word that means «fighter» in your country is?

They're optimistic

I want to add and share two expressions that are very important to me: **optimistic and enthusiastic people**.

What is optimism?

Optimism is the attitude or tendency to see and judge things in their most positive or favorable aspect. The word optimism comes from Latin, *optimum*, which means «the best.»

The term optimism was used for the first time by the German philosopher Gottfried Wilhelm Leibniz in his work *Essays of Theodicy on the Goodness of God, the Freedom of Man and the Origin of Evil* (Amsterdam, 1710), and then by the philosopher and writer Voltaire in *Candide.* As such, optimism is an attitude that allows one to positively value each circumstance lived by the individual, allowing them to face the obstacles with courage and perseverance.

An optimist has a positive attitude, and that is good, but the enthusiast makes things happen.

Enthusiasm

What is enthusiasm?

Enthusiasm is the encouragement produced by something that captivates or is admired. For the Greeks, «enthusiasm» means «have a god within oneself.» At present, it's known «enthusiasm» to what moves to carry out a transformative action, favor a cause or develop a project.

Happiness and inner well-being are also associated with enthusiasm, which can arise naturally and spontaneously, without concrete or specific reasons.

During the happy, joyful, and positive times in our lives, we usually face the day-to-day with spontaneous enthusiasm, which seems to be our personality trait. There are several ways to understand the concept of enthusiasm; for example, the word is linked to the term inspiration since it manifests in a particular and, many times, unpredictable way in everyone. Enthusiasm is awakened by means and forms different in each of us.

Come on, let's make things happen; it isn't enough to be optimistic.

This reminds me of a sales champion that told me one day: «I am going to bring out the Hulk in me,» and that's how it was. By bringing it out, it also comes out that we can transform what we want by altering energy. We positively infect every-one. It consists of adding an extra in the things we do. Always up, as we advance.

Recommendation: Don't let negative people or black clouds influence us, as they're often called. Let's help them become enthusiasts; let's make our team work to be proactive, optimist and have a transformative force. One spoiled fruit can contaminate all other ripe and green ones.

I invite you to stop and observe each of the images in this book; let's think, imagine and relate everything we have seen in this book.

They're resilient

Today the word is trendy due to the COVID-19 pandemic. It means to be a person with the ability to adapt to adverse situations. As you'll see in this book, I discovered the secret of selling and motivation in a difficult situation. That helped me overcome crises and adapt to the environment.

Resiliency is the capacity of human beings to adapt to adverse situations positively. Similarly, resiliency is the capacity to succeed acceptably in society, despite stress or hardship that involves a serious risk of negative results. It's also defined as a competitive process, where a person must adapt positively to complex situations.

«Resiliency» comes from the Latin verb *resilio*, which means «to go back, jump back, highlight, and bounce.» The word «resiliency,» in physics and chemistry, refers to the capacity of the steel to recover its initial shape, despite the blows it may receive and the efforts made to deform it. We can compare it with our lives, if we're pliable against different situations and difficulties.

Neuroscience considers that the most resilient people have more emotional equilibrium against stressful situations, as they can handle the pressure better. This gives them a sensation of control against events and more capacity to undertake challenges. This capacity to resist is tested in stressful situations, as the unexpected loss of a loved one, mental or physical abuse or mistreatment, long-term illnesses, emotional abandonment, failure, natural disasters, or extreme poverty. It may be said that resiliency is integrity beyond resistance.

Therefore, it could be said that resiliency is «a dynamic cause that results in positive adaptation in the context of a great misfortune,» as noted by AMR Piaggio and other sources consulted.

This is because it isn't considered a capacity but a process that encompasses a lot of factors. When a person is going through a challenging or extreme situation, it's influenced by the family, environment, economic state, friendships, and, of course, the person itself.

It's also essential to know the concept of «change resistance» to overcome adversity and adapt to present and future changes in the best possible way.

Change resistance

What is the resistance to change?

Some people develop a total resistance to change, while others are practically fans of the novelty it implies. In any case, life itself is change. Therefore, it's essential to develop a high level of tolerance that allows dealing with transformations without affecting our balance, despite the environment.

Kübler-Ross, E. and Kessler, D. (2007) proposed an emotional cycle that people follow during grief periods, but it also applies in any circumstance of life we refuse to accept.

The first phase is called the shock stage. We don't usually react at this stage, so others think we have readily accepted the transformation, but in reality, our emotional system is «frozen.» Then comes the denial stage. At this stage, we deny the change; it means to close our eyes in front of reality and any evidence that transformation is necessary or is happening. Typically, we continue our lives as if nothing has happened, with the naïve pretensions that the need to change will disappear. After this, seeing that there is no going back in change, we move to the anger stage, discomfort and rage at the situations that aren't as we want them. After this, we enter the negotiation stage. We still haven't accepted the change in this phase but are trying to find a «solution» to continue avoiding it. From this, we move to depression, in which we accept that change is unavoidable. Finally, the test stage comes, in which the change resistance starts to wane as we realize we need to react. In this acceptance stage, we're aware that change is the only constant in life.

If we think that the things we have done through the years will continue to work in the same way and that there aren't motives to change, we'll resist any transformation. Fear of the unknown, the uncertainty that generates any change, no matter how small, and wanting to stay in our comfort zone, are the principal reasons for resistance to change.

It's a factor of resistance to change that arises as a false mechanism of defense when we're invaded by a fear sense that translates as a danger alert. When we think that we don't have the abilities, competencies, or necessary strength to face transformation, we often unconsciously react by resisting the transition.

In short, we must develop adaptative skills to the changes that the environment undergoes. We can't resist these changes, but we can devise new ways to succeed, to achieve our goal. If the road doesn't allow us to advance, let's make a trail or short-cut and continue working on what we want.

Inspiring quotation

Insanity is doing the same thing, over and over again, but expecting different results.

Albert Einstein

What do you think? Is it essential to develop adaptative skills?

They're humble. They know their strength and weaknesses but don't brag about them.

What is being humble for you?

Humility is the integrity of recognizing one's own limitations and weaknesses by turning them into strength. It could be said that humility is the absence of arrogance; it's a key characteristic of simple people who don't feel more important or better than others, regardless of how much they have achieved in life.

The word humility can be used as a synonym of poverty, of lack of resources. Religions usually associate humility with recognition of divine superiority. For Buddhism, humility is the awareness of the path that must be followed to be free from suffering.

From philosophy, Immanuel Kant affirms that humility is the central virtue in life, as it provides a proper perspective of morality. For Friedrich Nietzsche, on the other hand, humility is a farce of virtue that hides the deceptions a person keeps within.

For me, humility isn't a synonym of poverty but the absence of ego, and it's excellent quality. It's to set an example by doing things right, without accusing anyone, without any protagonism, leaving great teachings. One of the strengths that humility leaves us is knowing our weaknesses. We can't be good at everything we do, but if you know your shortcomings in an area, you'll be able to recognize the strength of others. From it, teamwork will allow you to complement the competencies. This way, with the help of others, you'll achieve what you want: teamwork. It doesn't matter your socioeconomic level, but you as a person. You deserve whatever you dream of: make it happen.

When pride cometh, then cometh shame: but with the lowly is wisdom.

(Proverbs 11:2)

They learn

They're worried about learning. Every day, our professional salesperson, entrepreneur, merchant, business owner, professional, or homemaker has a learning desire to help them be better, capable. We are curious; we hunger the good things, taste knowledge.

Inspiring quotation

There is only one good, knowledge. And one evil, ignorance.
Socrates (470-399 BC)
Greek philosopher

An investment in knowledge always pays the best interest.
Benjamin Franklin (1706-1790)
American statesman and scientist

The sovereignty of man lieth hid in knowledge.
Francis Bacon (1561-1626)
British philosopher and statesman

True freedom is achieved with knowledge. Speaking of the world of sales and business, whoever has the more expertise presents better arguments, that is, they have a privileged position before their prospective client, as it allows them to wield a convincing critical tool, which is the truth of what they think about their product or service, so they transmit it and are successful. Ultimately, they dominate their business, but as knowledge grows, they never stop learning.

Do you care about learning? Are you curious?

They're a strategist

A person capable of implementing and developing a tactic or set of plans to achieve a goal, that is, they have an action plan to obtain results in the best way.

A strategy is a plan to solve a problem. It consists of a series of planned actions that help make decisions and obtain the best results. It aims to meet goals following a particular way of action. A strategy can include a series of tactics that are specific measures to achieve one or more goals.

The Art of War teachings on strategies:

Written around the 6th century BC, the manual created by the general and strategist Sun Tzu has inspired over the centuries many historical figures as Hannibal, Machiavelli, Napoleon, even well-known people in our time.

This book is about the importance of having a strategy in any area of life. According to Sun Tzu, without a plan, we're in the hands of chance and walk with total security towards defeat, «this is the difference between those who have a strategy and those who haven't» he adds.

Some of his most memorable quotes are:

«To subdue the enemy without fighting is the acme of skill.»

«The enemy who acts in isolation, lacks strategy, and takes adversaries lightly, will inevitably end up being defeated.»

«When the enemy is relaxed, make them toil.»

«If you know the enemy and know yourself, you need not fear the result of a hundred battles.»

«If you use the enemy to defeat the enemy, you will be powerful wherever you go.»

«Those skilled in war can make themselves invincible but cannot cause an enemy to be certainly vulnerable.»

Define with your own words what is to be a strategist:

Indeed, someone who sets a plan and strategy can achieve their goals quickly, reducing the difficulties.

They succeed

They succeed today and in the future. Their effort is compensated first by feeling satisfied with the well done work and, of course, with the obtained results.

We're people with everything we need to succeed in life, even when we think it isn't true. To succeed in life, first, we must define our goal and, if we take it to our personal level, we must know our priorities to reach as high as possible and achieve our target and then overcome it. Success is personal; it's mine. Let's name the things we have achieved, family, friends, academic milestones, of business, in life, among others, it's a triumph achieved, that you did and nobody else, and now define your next one.

The following recommendations will allow you to succeed in whatever you propose. First, you must know what you want; it's your triumph (we'll speak more about this in the secret of motivation). The phrase «wanting is power» fits accordingly here; it's a principle that means that we can obtain it if we put energy in the achievement of a trophy. This sense emphasizes the importance of the **will**, **zeal**, **commitment**, and **perseverance** to project ourselves to reach our goal. Therefore, this principle is also used to remind us that success doesn't come alone, but it's necessary to align our will with our aspirations. I affirm in my life: what I want, I can; it's my triumph.

For you, what is to succeed in life?

What is your triumph, or what are you searching for?

CHAPTER 2

THE MATERIAL OF A PROFESSIONAL SALESPERSON

What is a professional salesperson, entrepreneur, merchant, doctor, religious person, entrepreneur, or homemaker made of?

Vocation

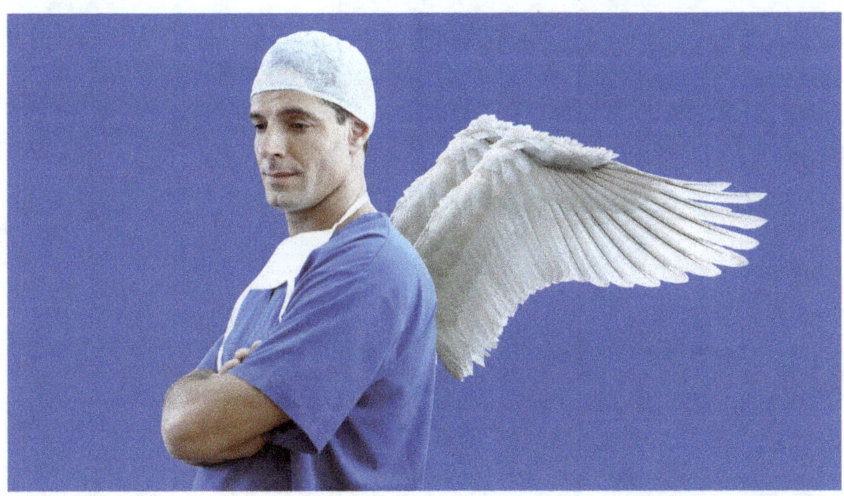

Vocation is the desire to start a career, a profession, or any other occupation or activity when not all the necessary skills or knowledge have been acquired. Another form of vocation is married life since two people join to form one being, which means they help each other. However, to find our vocation, we must see around us, our environment, our neighbors. Vocation is found when we discover what others need from us. The best example is a good mother or father who watches over their children.

When we talk about vocation, we refer to service, giving, and not necessarily giving what we're but doing what others need. This is notably related to our commercial or sales activity.

From the Spanish word for vocation, *vocación*, I'll make an acrostic:

Valor (Value)
Objetivo (Objective)
Conocimiento (Knowledge)
Amor (Love)
Carisma (Charm)
Imaginación (Imagination)
Organización (Organization)
Naturalidad (Naturalidad)

Value

V for valor (value)

Value is a broad concept that may refer to a character, a dignity, or a personal talent. Values are internal and subjective; they represent what we feel most strongly and that guides our behavior. Values control our conduct, and principles take care of the consequences of that behavior.

We all have talents, but we must discover and develop them. Have courage as a life principle. The most significant degree of this talent would be to become virtuous.

According to the Catholic Church Catechism (CCC), Virtue is «a habitual and firm disposition to do good. It allows people not only to perform good deeds but to give the best of themselves. With all their sensitive and spiritual forces, a virtuous person tends toward the good, seeks it, and chooses it through concrete actions.»

Objectives

O for objetivos (objectives)

What is an objective?

An objective or purpose is a goal or aim whose actions or operations are directed towards a specific plan. Everything we do has a purpose, an ultimate direction that drives us toward where we want to go; in short, a goal is the sum of the steps to achieve it. From our capacity or not to achieve it'll depend on our measure of success or failure.

Objectives are usually set before acting since it's convenient to know the way before starting to walk. We can only determine the best path to take if we see what the goal is. This way, objectives are part of planning in any field, especially in business and sales.

Academic research, feasible projects, business plans, or military strategies always have in mind the goal set beforehand and, therefore, seek to determine the most convenient way to make it real. Once achieved, there'll be a new one to continue with our new business goals and objectives.

Our goal must be clear. The most important is how to achieve it, that is, its execution.

The more straightforward questions you must ask and answer are: «What?,» «When?,» «Where?,» and «How?.»

Define your objective by answering these questions:

What?

What do I want to achieve with my goal or objective. Quantify.

When?

In what time I want to achieve my goal or objective.

Where?

In which place, location, channel, market do I want to achieve my goal or objective.

How?

How I'll achieve my objective, with what plan, strategy, product, or service.

I urge you to study PDCA continual improvement process and ISO 9000 standards to complete, review and follow up on our objectives or plans.

The PDCA cycle, devised by Walter Shewhart and developed by Edwards Deming, has been used since the fifties of the 20th century to the present day in quality management processes. In fact, the name «PDCA» was coined by participants in their classes that optimized the Shewhart cycle to «plan, do, check, act.» Deming used the word «study» instead of «check,» as the term stresses the idea of analyzing results instead of only verifying what had changed. However, the approach is currently known as the PDCA cycle because it's designed to be completed and repeated cyclically.

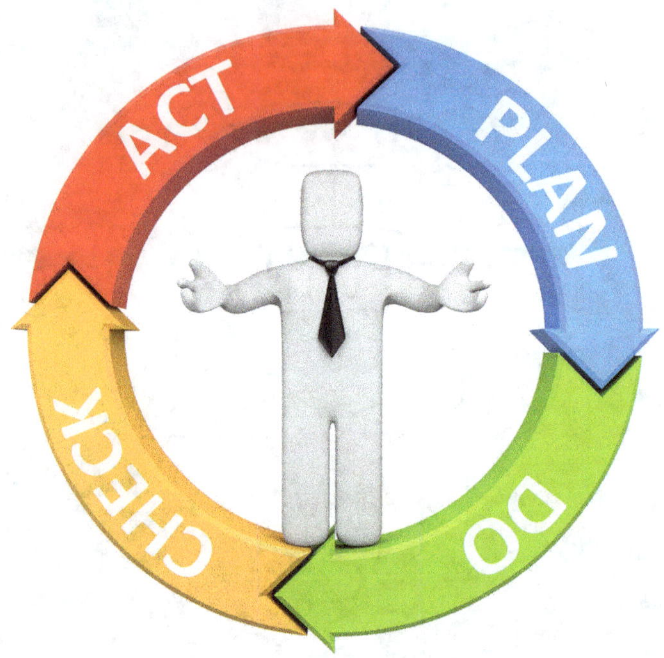

PLAN, DESIGN (PLAN) refers to establishing **objectives and necessary processes to achieve results in terms of the client's requisites and the policies of the organization**, according to the development of the activity. The tasks of the process are created, necessary to achieve the expected result. The methodology, activities, and tasks specific to the plan must be considered when settling the actions on the desired effect. It's called (**preventive actions**).

1) Define the goal or objective.
2) Define the method to achieve them.
3) Educate and train.
4) What to do and how to do it?

The method of the secret of selling

I'm going to say already that the method of the secret of selling
is **contact vs. sales**. The topic of the secret of selling will be

discussed in depth later in this book. It'll allow you to determine your action plan always to obtain the best results.

To do is the **how**; it refers to executing the plan based on a methodology, doing the tasks and activities. It's encouraged and recommended always to do pilot plans and then entirely implement the improvement actions.

Do the job. Execute

CHECK or **STUDY** is to follow up on the execution, measure the plan and the product, report the results, and evaluate the fulfilled plan's effectiveness.

Evaluate and verify the results of the tasks executed

ACT is to take actions to continue improvement and return to the step of calling to execute corrective measures, that is, eliminate the detected errors so as to improve in this way.

The PDCA will also help to correct mistakes and avoid them in the future. At this point, the PDCA becomes something more than an approach to solve problems; but it can also give valuable and essential information on different processes of your team or organization. The PDCA cycle is an adaptable strategy. This adaptability makes it scaleable, as it can be adapted to any situation and group of any size, even one person.

While the application of some management and problem resolution approaches may require a lot of time and resources, the adaptability of PDCA makes it applicable in most cases. PDCA is an excellent option if you wish to improve your or your team's work processes constantly. However, the systematic and incremental approach of PDCA means the changes happen gradually.

The strength of PDCA is in its capacity to continuously identify the problems to debug later and find optimal planning methods.

Let's keep spelling this wonderful word: **vocation**.

Knowledge

C for conocimiento (knowledge)

Knowledge is a discerning exercise, that is, understanding reality by obtaining valuable information through reason, intellect, and wisdom. Then, it refers to the result of the learning process. The word knowledge has several meanings. In a broad sense, it refers to the accumulated information about a subject. Still, specifically, knowledge means a set of skills, abilities, thought processes, and information acquired by a person, whose function is to help them explain reality, solve problems, and guide their behavior.

The word knowledge comes from Old English *knowleche*, formed by *knowen* that means «to know, recognize» and the suffix *leche*.

We must say, however, that the building of knowledge process is highly complex and includes many variables, which is why several schools are dedicated to the formulation of a knowledge theory. Some of the authors that have studied this phenomenon are Jean Piaget, through his theory of cognitive development, and Lev Vygotsky, through his sociocultural theory.

We must say then, dear readers, that striving to acquire knowledge of the topics that concern and delight us must be a daily obligation to structure our vocation.

The question to answer is, what do we sell? Of course, responding means knowing our service or product perfectly. It's a severe mistake, evident in some commercial teams, that a seller doesn't know the service or product offered in detail.

Love

A for amor (love)

Live life with love; to people, nature, what we do.

I encourage people to read about love, which must be one of the fundamental pillars of life at any level of human development.

The passion with which we do things will be reflected constantly; it'll allow us to have better results. Put skin to your feelings, existence, and relationships.

Regardless of the religion or belief, I believe that one of the most important messages for humanity was the one Jesus left us about love: «A new commandment I give unto you, That ye love one another; as I have loved you, that ye also love one another» (John 13:34).

A mother's love and a good father toward their children are the most significant forms of love. Those of us who love our children know the meaning of love. This feeling of love must be taken into our daily life and our relations with people. Let's be generous, and we'll never lack anything. Don't worry so much about the future; live the present. We have the tools to achieve what we want. We have a love for people and what we do.

Let's keep spelling the word **vocation**.

Charm

C for carisma (charm)

Charm is a quality people possess to enchant and convey sympathy to others. Even if it's considered a natural gift, since it's associated with a positive assessment of oneself, it's also true that this quality can be developed and encouraged in people by working on their self-esteem, self-confidence, and personal appreciation.

Therefore, it's fundamental to work on self-love to be charismatic, to please people as we're. Let's be ourselves. Indeed you're extremely pleasant, and yet you aren't aware of it.

Are you a pleasant person?

Know that I don't have any doubts that you're a wonderful and special person. You're unique; no two are alike in this world, I can assure you.

Imagination

I for imaginación (imagination)

The imagination is a superior creative process that allows the person to manipulate intrinsically generated information to create a representation that the senses can perceive. To that effect, imagination is related to the perceiving process.

It's an abstract process; it doesn't need an object present in reality. It uses memory to manipulate information and relate it, so that doesn't depend on the actual state of the organism or thing that surrounds us. In other words, the imagination takes elements perceived and experimented with before and transforms them into new stimuli or realities.

The studies on imagination date back from ancient times, but psychological and neuroscientific research has taken imagination as a challenge towards the end of the 20th and the beginning of the present century. Joint neuroimaging and conductual methods have allowed us to glimpse how the brain imagines.

Psychologists have studied imagination as creativity and artistic expression and its cognitive form, so they have concluded that it's based on the same cognitive processes as rational thinking.

Have you seen the importance of imagination in perceiving what surrounds us? Watch out for positive imagination that puts us where we must and deserve to be. Imagination is like our rational thinking that becomes a reality when we materialize what we create and imagine possible. You can't imagine the level of satisfaction that produces! Let's imagine and make it true. Positive imagination is an ally that must accompany us through our lives; that cycle of visualizing, materializing, achieving, and keep imagining again will make the difference.

Let's continue with the word **vocation** and the letters that compose it.

Organization

O for organización (organization)

Organizations are different administrative bodies that are grouped under diverse modalities: cooperatives, companies, societies, etc.; that is, they're systems created to achieve goals and shared objectives that have a life of their own thanks to the support of the people that integrate them.

An organization is the means that help us achieve our goals, but also the word refers to order, that allows us to fulfill all our daily activities. From the moment we wake up until we go to bed, we must be organized, structured, and focused.

Let's be organized.

Naturalness

N for naturalidad (naturalness).

Naturalness is to act spontaneously and with simplicity in the interaction and way of proceeding.

In short, to succeed in all our activities, we must have a **vocation** in what we do, serve others, love people, don't forget this word, that is my suggestion.

Do you agree?

What would be your criteria?

CHAPTER 3

HOW TO WIN A CLIENT?

How to win a customer?

- Help them discover the benefits they expected.
- Make them appreciate your work.
- Make them feel good about themselves for having bought.
- Satisfy their needs, tastes, and demands.
- Ensure that they feel good at any time, that receive from you good attention and service.

With emotion, you'll touch the heart of people.

Being unique, that is, original.

Remarkable: famous in the experience.

- Who am I?
- Emphasis: identifying the client's needs.
- Communicating in both ways.
- Negotiation instead of manipulation.
- After-sales service.
- Sales are relationships; you're selling to people.
- The first impression is the one that counts.
- Reach out and relate with your client, show them honestly what interest you, with a simple conversation, like a friend's.
- Connect with their heart, dreams, and desires.
- Be the best at knowing your business or product.
- Be confident and convey it to your entire environment safely.
- Highlight your principles and values.
- You're unique; no two people are the same in this world.
- Really listen, be interested in asking about your customer's needs.
- Tell a success story of a client of yours, tell your own experience.

How to win many customers?

> Give importance to everyone.
> Take a sincere interest in others.
> Never argue openly.
> Listen carefully and let others speak.
> Respect the ideas of others.
> Force yourself to learn proper names.

If you want to make money, use these recommendations.

What do you think?

Role

Salesperson, entrepreneur, merchant, businessperson, homemaker roles.

Roles are functions assigned to people so, in specific situations or circumstances, they act or behave according to a set of guidelines to satisfy a series of expectations. An individual plays a social role in certain circumstances according to a group of behavioral patterns established by society. So, the social role would be what is expected of an individual's behavior in their social environment. Social roles determine how individuals relate to each other and with specific social institutions, as family, education, religion, company, politics, economics, etc.

Each social institution is governed by specific standards or guidelines that the individual must respect, not to be rejected or excluded. A behavior other than the normal generates, in general, certain social sanctions.

What should be our role?

To **produce**, to **sell**. Therefore, we must sell at any moment or circumstance. The first thing is to become aware that I own and am responsible for the production. I don't need a person that makes me move; I move by myself because I have goals and objectives to achieve. Help and teamwork are welcomed, but my role is my responsibility, no matter the position within the organization, that is, if I'm a salesperson, manager, director, entrepreneur, or businessperson.

They must think about their goals and objectives. Take advantage of the business opportunities, as they must pay off for you and your loved ones. If you gain by results, move, win, be a champion. If you think this way, you'll always be a winner.

Let's be our boss, businessperson, or entrepreneur. It doesn't matter if you're an employee because you'll be one of the best within the company if you have that attitude. This will ensure growth. It isn't just about thinking and saying, but demonstrating with facts, my dear friends.

I remember that I had to be an entrepreneurial businessman. I didn't have the opportunity to be an employee, although I fulfilled my duty as one in the areas assigned to me. My way of leading has always been as a teammate, with the support and help I can give my co-workers and friends. I founded a programmed savings company around 1996, with some partners who to this day still remain as such. It's an almost unknown business globally, different from credit and cash purchase of goods and services. In 2003, I had the opportunity to buy a similar company, which I founded with the same partners, but that celebrated fifty years of founded in May of 2021. In one opportunity, I told the biggest shareholder: «Maybe if I had met you in 1996, I could have been one of your best business advisors.» I bring this to tell you that life gives you roles, or we search for them; but without a doubt, the best is to find the position we like the most.

I always recommend that we have the mentality of an entrepreneur, no matter if you're a civil servant or dependent; this will take you to the top positions. Who doesn't like to be surrounded by interesting, wonderful, and skilled people who can teach us so much? I think that the professional champions with team spirit make things happen and everything more manageable.

Do you agree?

CHAPTER 4

THE SECRET OF MOTIVATION

What motivates you to move?

I have asked this question to maybe a thousand people in my training to sales personal, teams in general in all the areas of my company and other people, and they always answer: «A lot of money,» «family,» «money,» «education,» or «well-being.» Motivation is a fascinating topic; I'll now share with you the secret of motivation I have discovered for myself.

What is motivation?

Motivation is the action and effect that makes us react like people. It's the motive or reason that causes the performance or omission of activity, which invites us to move, be active, and desire what we want to achieve.

According to psychology and philosophy, motivation implies internal states that direct the organism towards determined goals or purpose.

Motivation can be divided into intrinsic and extrinsic. All these factors can be increased or diminished according to the environment surrounding the individual.

Thus, the intrinsic factors depend on the meaning given by the person to what they do. While it's true that the extrinsic factors also rely on the meaning given by the person, these can radically change easily. At the same time, the intrinsic requires a work of assimilation more appropriate to the individual's mind.

Intrinsic factors deal with people's desires to do things because they're considered essential or attractive.

Intrinsic motivation has been studied since the seventies and can be defined as the self-desire to search for new things and take on challenges to test or dare one's ability, observe and acquire more knowledge. Intrinsic motivation has been proven in experimental studies about animal behavior. It's a natural motivational tendency, and it's a critical element in physical, social, and cognitive development.

According to the self-determination theory of Ryan and Deci (2002), intrinsic motivation can be divided into knowledge, achievement, and stimulation.

On the other hand, extrinsic motivation refers to developing an activity to achieve the desired goal and is opposed to intrinsic motivation. External forces on the individual generate extrinsic motivation. In this kind of motivation, the more complicated question to answer is where a person finds the necessary inspiration to carry out a task and continue to strive persistently. Generally, extrinsic motivation is used to achieve results that a person couldn't obtain from intrinsic motivation.

Both extrinsic and intrinsic motivation can be presented as positive or negative, whose assessment will depend on their consequences. Positive encouragement is sought by a person looking for a reward. Instead, in negative motivation, the only force driving a person is to forego an unpleasant consequence.

Burrhus Frederic Skinner believed that the best way to understand an individual's behavior entirely is to investigate the causes of an action and its consequences. Operant conditioning, his most known theory, is a conditioned learning method based on rewards and punishments for behavior. The changes in conduct are the results of a person's reaction in a given setting or environment.

The push motivations are those in which people are stimulated towards their goals to achieve something. However, this motivation isn't entirely functional, as it's easy to be discouraged when facing obstacles in the way.

In the pull motivations, it isn't the desire to achieve a goal but the objective that pulls us toward it. Thus, this motivation can generate a desire when external influences enter the scene.

Instead, the incentive theory refers to a boost or reward to do something. They can be tangible or intangible and are given, usually, after the corrected action or behavior happens again.

This incentive theory, followed by Skinner, refers to radical behaviorism, which means the people's actions will always have social repercussions. This theory differs from others related to motivation, like drive.

In incentive theory, stimuli attract a person to them.

Related to motivation, we'll find the content theory, one of the first motivation theories. Since this theory is centered on the importance of things that motivate us, it's also related to the needs theory. In other words, it tries to identify our necessities and how they're associated with motivation to satisfy them.

Moreover, Maslow's theory has been extensively discussed. According to Maslow, people are motivated due to unsatisfied necessities.

As you can see, motivation is a subject that has been studied from different approaches; we have reviewed some theories about it to know what makes us move towards our goals.

After reading all this, do you know what the secret to motivation is?

Many say: «My motivation is the money.» I ask you: What good is the money if they don't know what they want, what motivates them? Money, family, or education alone don't encourage.

I discovered that what motivated me was to have a packed fridge. One day I arrived home as I was starting my venture; I opened my fridge and realized it looked like a utility bill: water and electricity. Since then, I have told myself that it would never be empty again. Therefore, I had to move.

For me, the secret of motivation is to know what I want, how long until I achieve it, how to accomplish it, and through what means I'll get it. It matches the basic questions I asked to develop a plan: What? How? Where? And, When? Of course, we must also be very clear, why do I want this **triumph**? Why do I want this **specific** goal? Will it have the best consequences for the people I care about as my family or loved ones and me?

To know what you want. Because if you know what you want, you'll move to reach it and will always be motivated, no matter what.

Excuse me, my motivating friends of commercial teams. I recognize the excellent work you do, as you fuel us, make us jump, dance, laugh, find our potentials, learn new things… as good as going to a party that leaves us happy. But friends, if we don't know what we want, that happiness will disappear soon. The best way to have high-octane gas, sun, wind, and energy are to know what you want. I call this essential and lasting self-motivation. There is no storm to stop us.

If you answered money to the previous question, why money?

If you said family, why move around for the family? To give them what?

If you said education, which education and when?

It means you must **set** your life **goals in a specific way**.

What motivates you? Answer the basic questions. Always be encouraged, succeed and stay motivated.

If I fulfill my role because I'm highly self-motivated and know what I want, nobody and nothing will stop me. We're like a train or a rocket: nothing discourages us because we know what we want. The hard part, friends, is to understand what we want because if we're sure and clear of it, a passion for what we do will be born, and we'll forget the word fatigue in our lives.

I have set a goal. Besides, I'm a professional salesperson, well trained, know my product or service, and know what I want; therefore, I'll only succeed in life.

How do you build success?

The success of the advisor, entrepreneur, businessperson, employee.

The first question a great professional salesperson or entrepreneur must ask is to know the utility I want to receive from my work? Without this becoming an unattainable dream, but a tangible goal.

Climb your own ladder, step by step; live one day at a time. You'll get where you want to go faster than you think.

CHAPTER 5

THE SECRET OF SELLING

Before we start the main topic of the book, I want to tell you a personal story. In 2002 and 2003, Venezuela lived an economic strike, a challenging and extreme situation that I or, instead, all Venezuelans lived. I'm Venezuelan and Colombian, and I also would like to be a citizen of the world.

At the time, the oil or economic strike in Venezuela, also called national or general strike, consisted of paralysis in all working and economic activities of a broad and indefinite nature against the Venezuelan government, presided over by

Hugo Chávez. This strike was promoted mainly by the business union *Fedecámaras* and the labor unions, *Confederación de Trabajadores de Venezuela* (CTV), supported by the opposition political parties and most Venezuelan population.

The reason behind it was that the Chávez government was considered undemocratic, and the legislative packages imposed by the government were unconstitutional. For this, *Fedecámaras* called for a twelve-hour national strike on December 10, 2001, an action supported by CTV, the country's main labor union. I would say it was a case study never seen before on a global scale: businesspersons and workers united for the same cause. From there, many opposition leaders and the vast majority -from my point of view- called for Chávez's resignation, an always rejected request.

When President Chávez didn't accept the businessperson's, the union's, opposition parties', and the people's demands -which consisted of withdrawing the legislative package and not imposing military personnel in the state oil company-, a first twenty-four-hour strike was called on December 9, 2001, then a second strike on April 9, 2002, that practically became indefinite until 2003.

This strike was also supported by employees of PDVSA, who stopped working and rejected the new board of directors Chávez had appointed in the industry, made up by external people, without the knowledge of the processes their operations managed.

On April 11, while the strike continued, the people, in a massive march against the government, decided to go to the Miraflores Presidential Palace, which provoked a confrontation against the pro-government members who were at the place. That pressured Chávez for two days for his resignation. The instability didn't cease, and unfortunately, many lives were lost, and several street confrontations between *Chavistas* and *anti-Chavistas*, almost daily in most of the main cities in the country, especially the capital, Caracas. The positions of both sides became even more radicalized. This way, the country became almost completely paralyzed.

This scenario marked the decline of PVDSA. The performance of the state oil company was severely affected in the following years, as it lowered its production and the number of occupational accidents increased. Most people staged *cacerolazos* every night.

To give you an idea of what this situation was, almost everything was closed: supermarkets, restaurants, shopping centers, which, from my point of view, was more severe than what we're experiencing with the COVID-19 pandemic. There was no gasoline, no food; the streets were empty, everything looked like an end-of-the-world movie. The news showed what was happening everywhere: riots and deaths.

At that time, I was the commercial director of *Consorcio Fonbienes, CA,* in Venezuela. The strike fractured many small, medium, and large companies, so they had to declare bankruptcy. After six months of the strike, the company may also have gone bankrupt. However, the entire work team was committed. We were supportive and reduced expenses and salaries, but we had to act on the matter because we were already reaching a critical stage. We decided that the commercial managers who wanted to open to do it, and those who don't, to continue with the strike. So, two of the fifty-five we had opened. One sold 125 contracts and the other, 98. I asked myself: «What is the secret?» I confess that the world had ended for me, my friends. Maybe now, with the pandemic, you have this feeling too, but don't worry, stay busy. This COVID-19 allowed me to write my first book, which you have so kindly accompanied me to read and write to confirm the secret of selling and motivation.

Usually, when I ask this question, almost no one answers it with certainty or precision. As a rule, the most common answer given is: «Satisfy the customers' needs.» It's pretty simple. The hardest is to apply it or execute it, have discipline, and measure the results.

We realized that based on the **face-to-face prospecting** -we called it that, at the time- these commercial teams had reached a high effectiveness index.

Prospecting has always been mentioned in sales, but not as the secret. The remedy we found in the face of the crisis was to prospect. We measured the effectiveness and realized it was around 11 %.

This formula saved us, which quickly activated the goals that had to be implemented in each commercial team. Starting from this foundation and with a professional team of sales highly trained that apply everything we have seen in this book, they'll surely obtain higher rates than those I proposed to our commercial units, which was 10 % at the time.

When everything went back to normal (over a year later), we set prospecting goals, and the results per advisor and team were enough. Another recommendation I made at the moment was to stop watching negative news. Remember: the world had ended for me, but I came back and stopped seeing the black cloud.

I bring you a table we made at the time, specifically in 2002. Now COVID-19 happened in 2020. How curious, right?

I called this file an objective, sales, and results simulator.

Setting objectives and planning. Simulator.

INDIVIDUAL GOAL

• INDIVIDUAL GOAL:	**120 CONTRACTS**
• REQUIRED NUMBER OF CONTACTS IN A YEAR:	1.200
• NUMBER OF MONTHLY CONTACTS:	100
• SALES TEAM:	1
• CONTACT PER SELLER PER MONTH:	96
• MANDATORY DAILY CONTACT:	4
• IDEAL EFFECTIVENESS BY CONTACT:	10 %
• ESTIMATED MONTHLY SALE:	10
• TOTAL CONTRACTS IN ONE YEAR:	120

TEAM GOAL

• TEAM GOAL:	**1.200 CONTRACTS**
• REQUIRED NUMBER OF CONTACTS IN A YEAR:	144.000
• NUMBER OF MONTHLY CONTACTS:	12.000
• SALES TEAM:	120
• CONTACT PER SELLER PER MONTH:	96
• MANDATORY DAILY CONTACT:	4
• IDEAL EFFECTIVENESS BY CONTACT:	10 %
• ESTIMATED MONTHLY SALE:	1.200
• TOTAL CONTRACTS IN ONE YEAR:	14.400

From this model, the most important for you'll be to discover the individual effectiveness, the team's, sales channels, the business, or product to create your own sales simulator and objectives in your industry to execute and fulfill what is proposed.

In this book, we saw how to establish a goal and to verify its fulfillment. We learned about the method, contacts vs. sales (contact factory). Those who believe and apply what is in this book will do what is planned, and the result will depend on each of you.

I share with you the trade policy applied at that time:

Commercial base

The secret of the sale and consequence: face-to-face contacts + minimum effectiveness 10 % + tracking. (Cause and effect: sales).

The secret of portfolio persistence: clear sales preserve friendships and customers for life = our primary commercial channel referrals / 100 % effectiveness.

Main team rules

1) Sales quality.
2) Daily contacts execution is fulfilled.
3) Negative people are not accepted.

The world continues to change, but in these eighteen years, we have obtained good results with this formula of the secret of selling: face-to-face prospects vs. effectiveness equal sales. Selling was physical until very recently.

As I told you, our company called *Autofinanciera Colombia, SA,* will turn fifty years old in 2021. *Fonbienes Colombia, SA*, another of our companies, celebrates thirty-three years. *Fonbienes Peru* turns twelve, while *Fonbienes Venezuela*, twenty-four years.

Regarding our companies, I can tell you that, from my point of view, they stayed in the 20th century until recently. Most of the sales were made in shopping centers, some advertising campaigns in traditional communication media, referrals, and our commercial offices.

Around 2017 I moved to Medellín to coordinate a commercial team, and I realized that it was the same thing that I had been practicing for more than twenty-four years when I started with this activity: events, fairs, flyers, etc. And I told myself, «It can't be the same; there must be other ways to sell differently.» I began to explore the digital world, took digital courses in digital universities, invested on my own in a topic I'm now passionate about, started to advertise in social media, and made sales generated by them. Thus I discovered a wonderful and infinite world. The best about digital advertising is that at once, you have the information on the customer or interested person, who is called the lead in the digital world. If we compare it with the phone calls generated by a press advertising, it's a lot of difference.

Companies have had various transformations, mainly in the digital world, a process in which I have participated as an innovation leader. Since I devised a commercial application focused on our business sector, it was an exciting project because nothing was similar in the world. Now we're becoming more virtual and less on-site. The pandemic has forced us to be at home and work from there, a situation that makes it challenging to sell traditionally. To my surprise, the secret to digital selling is to generate leads, turn them into prospects, and do so from the comfort of the home or workplace. Face-to-face and virtual effectiveness are usually different; find it out for yourself.

The **basis** of the **secret** of the **sale** remains the same: more prospects, more contracts, or sales. Our effectiveness must also be measured. This will allow us to plan and achieve our goals. Of course, we must prepare ourselves to sell virtually in our commercial activity or in whatever we want to undertake. For this, it'll be essential to have virtual tools, create marketing procedures, and activate a sales process that generates trust and security.

I hope that this information will be advantageous and useful to move from now. We see restaurants, supermarkets, insurance companies, service companies, products that sell online. The world is changing, but the fundamentals of commercial selling remain the same.

What is prospecting?

The search for natural or legal persons interested in our product or service is a fundamental key to maximizing commercial success. Those companies that dedicate a large part of their energy searching for potential customers stand out remarkably since their success is multiplied compared to others who refuse to take advantage of this invaluable resource. To increase the chances of success, it's necessary to keep this list constantly updated, which is achieved through frequent communication through different media or channels such as advertising, word of mouth, or own commercial efforts. **The idea is to connect constantly with our audience;** that is, all our business energies must be focused on the secret of looking for potential customers called prospects.

Dear friends, nowadays, social media is an excellent lead generator. Then they'll meet them **at the moment** and turn them into prospects to close a sale.

So, **THE SECRET OF SELLING IS PROSPECTING.** Don't believe in apocalyptic information about the crisis; believe in yourself, in your product and service. Generate prospects, and the business closure will come, that is, sales. The secret of selling is direct contact between leads and our knowledge of the product or service, concretized in effectiveness and results. The primary key to selling is direct contact with the prospective customer, and its main ally of success is follow-up. We can have direct contact with our prospects through social media; let's use these platforms that shorten distances and connect us with the world.

It's important to note that your planning method must be based on generating leads and closing deals by measuring their effectiveness. We talked about this topic when we referred to the PDCA continuous improvement process. Know-how is our secret. Contacts vs. sales (contact factory).

SCHEME OF THE CONCEPTO OF SELLING:

FACTORY	FOCUS	MEDIUM	PURPOSES	RELATION
Contacts	Tracking-sale	Plan	Satisfied customers	Increase

The mathematical formula of the secret of selling

The mathematical formula of the secret of the sale is present as follows. For me, it's a magic formula that doesn't fail; apply it, and you'll see it.

My effectiveness: ER (effectiveness rate) = [S (sales) / P (prospects)]*100

Personal goals

ER (effectiveness rate) = (S/P) *100 ER: effectiveness rate.
S: Sales.
P: Prospects.

Knowing my effectiveness. Let's suppose I attended to seventy prospects and sold ten businesses in a month. What is my effectiveness?
ER = (10/70) * 100
ER = 14,28 % effectiveness rate

It means, ¿how many businesses or sales should close if prospect 100 in a month?
Sales = (Prospects * ER)
Sales = 100 prospects * 14,28 % (effectiveness rate) Sales = 14 sales
So, the formula of the secret of selling is:
S = (P * ER)

Personal goals

It's essential to make a sincere and uncomfortable analysis of your company, your product and/or service.

Do you feel at ease? Do you see a future? Do you think that you'll achieve what you want? These are difficult questions to answer, but we must dwell on them, think, and make life decisions. If you decide to stay where you are, you must **grow:** start now; if not, it's time to look for another opportunity.

David Gómez (2018), in his article *Las ventas no son un escampadero*, recommends we don't take our commercial or work activity as a «shelter»: «Many people see working in sales as a place to protect themselves while getting something else» (Blog Bien Pensado), and what they do is lose their lives by missing productive and existence opportunities.

What do I want? Do I believe in the product? Do I believe in the company? Where do I want to go with my current situation, with my budget?

First, discover your effectiveness.

My effectiveness: ER (effectiveness rate) = S (sales) / P (prospects) * 100

Once you have your effectiveness rate, apply the secret of selling formula S = (P * ER), take it to your business; this effectiveness rate means money for you.

Constantly remember what motivates you.

I invite you to find your effectiveness. What is yours?

Do you think 100 prospects are too much in a month?

If we divide 100 by 24 working days, **how much does it give us?**

You would have to prospect four a day.

Do you think it's too much?

How many effective working hours you must do daily attending prospects?

You should work the number of hours you determine in a day, but do it. Attend your leads and make sales.

Acquire this habit of discipline, and you'll tell me.

How to improve effectiveness?

First, believe in what you do, in your product and/or service. You must be aware and improve thanks to everything seen in this book. Remember the example of the athlete: we're commercial athletes, and we must practice every day.

This is the formula of the secret of selling. It's also the formula to plan a sales goal knowing the effectiveness per number of prospects. Ask yourself: How much do I want to earn? And, what should I do? Put in place an action plan.

A commercial director who knows the effectiveness of their teams and business channels will set achievable goals. To close businesses, you must go through the steps and add small closures to refute objections, generate acceptance, and, of course, payment.

CHAPTER 6

THE SALES PROCESS

I explain the sales process as a zipper. If we're missing one of its parts, what happens? That's right: it won't work. It'll be tough to close the trousers' zipper. It also occurs in the sales process we'll see next. If you miss some steps, you won't close the sale.

The steps of the sale (general process / adapt it to your business)

1. Planning. Weekly and daily planning. (Four daily leads, for example).

2. Pre-sales approach. Planning of contacts and interviews. (It can be by any means: digital or physical).
3. Approach. A cordial greeting to the customer, capture their attention and trust.
4. Presentation. Customer research: Who makes the decision? What does the customer want? What does the customer have?
5. Argumentation. Presentation of the benefits and advantages for the customer. The objective is to encourage desire, overcome objections, arouse interest by activating the five senses; have a sequence of advantages and benefits, demonstration, management of resistance to sale. Add small closures.
5. Closure. The goal is to make the sale. (Result: the purchase, payment).
6. After-sales. Provide a good service that generates new customers (continuous improvement, portfolio maintenance). The most challenging work has already been done, now do the easiest: keep your client and grow your portfolio.

The sales process is everything involved in the marketing of the product or service offered by the company; it's a guide prepared by the firm in which it must be specified, step by step, how the product or service will be offered and sold to the customer. A seller who follows a guide in the sales process will better understand the customer's needs. Understanding what the client is looking for makes it easier to highlight the positive points and differences that the product has and may interest them.

Knowledge of the product or service

Every salesperson must have a deep knowledge of the products and services that the organization offers. Believe in your company, product, service, or brand to transmit it with security and credibility.

Customer Prospecting

The second step of the sales process is the prospection of the client, that is, the first contact with the potential buyer. In this stage, the company must be clear about which audience it wants to attract or conquer as a client and develop strategies so that prospecting actions are directed towards them. Remember the secret of the sale.

Approach

Once we find our potential customers, we must think about how they'll meet the salesperson.

Presentation

I recommend knowing the customer: profile your prospect, who makes the decision? What does the customer want? **What do they have?** Argumentation, presentation of the benefits and advantages for the client. The goal is to encourage desire, overcome objections, arouse interest through the five senses, sequence of advantages and benefits, demonstration, resistance to selling management. Adding small closures means completing several **affirmations or agreements during our commercial presentation** with our potential or interested client and then completing the sale with the purchase of the product or service. It's very difficult for the person to say that they won't buy when they have agreed with you several times in your presentation. Analyze what the prospect has and offer what they can buy; you don't create any objections.

This reminds me that, at my house, I always have the last word when we're going to buy something, and my statement is very resounding; «Yes, my love.» So, the question is: Who makes the decision? Because it's fundamental to close a sale. As well as what do they have? And what does our prospective client need?

Closure or sale

Once small closures have been made in your presentation, the sum will give the closure of the sale, which is the payment or purchase.

After-sales

Let's refresh: provide a good service that generates new customers (continuous improvement, portfolio maintenance, etc.). The hard work has already been done, now do the easiest: keep your client and grow your portfolio.

We already know what the secret of selling is. The concern should be to generate contacts, leads (interested people) in our business, service, or product. This must be very **clear to us** because we must attend to them and close the deals. Sales will come alone according to our effectiveness. So don't worry and **focus on prospecting and increasing your effectiveness.**

A brother once asked me: «What is the secret of a commercial place to sell food,» and I told him what I had learned in a real estate broker course: «Location, location, and location.» But it's simple. While more people go through that space, you'll probably have more sales. The principle is the same: the secret. This is analyzed by all franchise businesses worldwide, but if you also boost your business in traditional media or digital marketing, you'll be adding to the secret. It works the same as what I told you about our vehicle sales because we do them in shopping centers. It's sought that many people go through our commercial point to be attended and thus close businesses or deals. The same happens in the physical, virtual, or digital worlds. Add the two commercial fields, and you'll have more results. Immortalize the secret of selling and motivation.

The world will continue to change, but the combination of the physical and the virtual in the world of sales will continue to exist. There will be physical, digital, and combined sales. At least, that's what I think will happen in the next twenty years. What any entrepreneur needs to know is that they must digitalize in the commercial area. If you don't, you'll be losing customers and be behind in today's competitiveness. See the consequences with COVID-19, which forced all companies to reinvent themselves in a short period of time.

My suggestion is that you worry about generating contacts, prospects, or leads. This is the secret of selling that you already know. Take care of them and close the business; use your skills and knowledge for it. Don't worry, act, and with this, any crisis will affect you less.

What do you think of the sales process?

Build your own sales process

CHAPTER 7

OBJECTIONS

Another topic I'm very passionate about is the handling of objections. Objections are statements from clients expressing disagreement with what the advisor claims.

Why do they appear? Because: the client doesn't understand what the advisor tells him; they don't know the product or service; aren't interested, or if they're, don't see the benefits; don't believe that the expense is justified; are unsure of the decision, and have resistance to change; believe their image will be affected; see it as an excessive expensive; don't have the resources;

don't have the autonomy or want to get rid of you, it's the wrong time, they don't like you; aren't interested in your company; want to measure you; wish to postpone the decision or don't find your argument convincing, etc. But it can also happen that you don't convey the security, the message, or you don't know your product or service.

Dear colleagues, for you, what are the main objections to your business?

Objections make the sales dynamic; they eventually come forward because you didn't foresee them.

Attitude to objections

Objections are welcome because they indicate how the sale is progressing, guide you on what is missing to close the deal and allow you to know how your customer thinks.

How to clarify objections? You must have criteria to add small closures in the presentation to achieve the total closing of the sale. Remember the example of the zipper.

Some ways:

- Asking directly. **Important:** you must be careful doing this question.
  √   Advantage: shows the true objection.
  √   Disadvantage: may affect the atmosphere of the negotiation.
- Trying to guess.
- Imagination.

You mustn't create objections

The Four No's

- I don't want to.
- I don't need to.
- I don't have a budget.
- I don't think the product or service is good.

It's important your perception ability, that nose. Don't downplay the objections.

Types of objections

Entry objections: they refer to necessity, product or service, yourself, the company, the immediate decision.

Behavior and handling

Avoid arguing; evaluate the objection and not the person. Put yourself in your customer's place, don't hurt their self-esteem, exempt them from guilt, and respond in a cordial tone. Allow the customer to speak and listen and think before answering. Assume the win-win position. Be concise in your answers. Talk with examples, facts, and data. Avoid irrelevant objections, don't be repetitive, don't magnify.

Resources for handling objections

The best weapons:

- Knowledge of yourself, your product, and your safety.
- Ability to analyze.
- Good judgment.
- Creativity.
- Positive mind.

Golden rules

- Listen to your client's objection.
- Reformulate it in your own words.
- Answer it correctly and safely.
- Verify acceptance (summation of closures) and close it. Don't be afraid.

The sale is today, not tomorrow

My recommendation is simple; list all the objections with your team about your business and create a plan of strong responses to each of the possible objections to refute them. This is an excellent tool that every commercial team must have without fail.

Closure of the sale or business

Recommendations:

1. Know about your product and/or service, advantages, and benefits.
2. Know your interested prospect customer.
3. What do they have (resources).
4. Who makes the decision.
5. What does your customer want (need).
6. Offer what your customer wants and can acquire.
7. Small closures or acceptance by your prospective customer in your sales presentation.
8. Sell, get paid. (Always ask in affirmative: How will you pay? Credit card, cash, transfer, or check).

What kind of executive am I?

Types of salespersons:

- Understanding.
- Agresive
- Advisor

Define what is to be understanding?

They're very good people, but unfortunately, they're problem buyers. They don't sell. They're interested in people but don't give commercial solutions.

What does an aggressive salesperson look like?

It reminds me of the old timeshare or used vehicle salespersons. They sell, but they can fall into sales for today and hunger for tomorrow; they aren't interested in the person but the deal. If there is no quality of purchase, there will be no portfolio of satisfied customers, which will make the job more complex every day. Of course, I want to highlight those people who do their job well in any activity, having the best of the two previous types of sellers (understanding and aggressive), those we call advisors.

What is being an advisor?

The advisor is interested in people. They have a vocation, are professional, apply everything we have seen in this book, are well trained, and sell because they believe in what they do and transmit it correctly, and they respect their work.

How should it be between these three types of sellers? Why?

CHAPTER 8

KNOWLEDGE SUMMARY

Please write:

What is the secret of motivation?

Know what you want. What do you want? The answer must come from our thoughts, soul, and spirit.

What is the secret of selling?

Prospect. Prospecting aims to create a list of interested people in our business and then contact them systematically to transform them into customers.

Mathematical formula of the secret of selling:

Sales equal prospects by effectiveness rate. S = (P*ER)

> S= Sales.
> P= Prospects.
> ER= Effectiveness rate.

What is sales effectiveness?

It's my effectiveness rate that comes from the sales made by the number of attended prospects.

My effectiveness: ER (effectiveness rate) = S (sales) / P (prospects) * 100

Example: I attended 100 prospects and closed 15 sales, then my effectiveness is 15 %.

What is prospecting?

It refers to locating the people interested in our business, product, or service to turn them into potential customers, attend them methodically, and then become buyers. Close the sale. Remember, sum the small closures.

What is to sell?

It's the action of closing a negotiation with quality, generating a payment or purchase by our potential or interested customer, based on our professional knowledge about our product or service, which creates and maintains a lasting business relationship.

I invite you to answer the questions with your own words to solidify the learning of this book and put it into practice in your commercial activity or business from now on.

CHAPTER 9

INCREASE OUR EFFECTIVENESS

We already know what the secret of motivation and selling is. Now it's up to us to increase the effectiveness of business closures.

Let's see how to increase our effectiveness

We're commercial professionals. Therefore, we must practice as athletes until we optimize our everyday effectiveness. I'll present you with some ideas for this.

Techniques for business advisors, entrepreneurs, businesspersons, for everyone

These are the different practices we must develop to perfect our closure technique and increase our effectiveness.

Explain them yourself and what would they be useful for:

Dramatizations:

It's acting as you were with a potential customer to master different commercial situations. Our commercial life is a stage theatre.

The mirror technique:

Make your business presentation in front of a mirror so you can see and evaluate yourself.

The dual test technique:

Rehearse with your teammates; the idea is to perfect and contribute together, highlighting our strengths and improving our weaknesses. Usually, it's done with two persons: one as a salesperson and the other as a buyer.

The technique of group corrections:

Some team members see our presentations, while the others, as spectators, suggest actions of improvement.

Monologue:

Perform a monologue, record, and listen to yourself, correct what you must.

Multiple dramatizations:

Several people are selling, and many are buying. The idea of these practices is to show the weaknesses to turn them into strengths through the suggestions made by the drama team.

Case review:

Review real commercial cases of sales made and not achieved to draw your own conclusions and improvement actions.

Voice changes:

Seek commercial support inside your teamwork; it happens when we haven't closed the sale with a potential customer. Sometimes, changing the voice is the solution to sell and see what we can improve.

Call testing:

Perform practice calls among the team members.

Virtual interviews:

Master virtual meetings or interviews through the existing digital applications.

Practice makes perfect and increases our security; it makes us more effective and efficient, so the more effective, the more sales per attended prospect. The popular saying we started this paragraph is used to encourage people to persevere in what they want to achieve. If your goal is to learn to sell or increase your effectiveness, you're advised to practice the recently commented resources every day for a certain amount of time. Any skill requires practice to be effective.

Efficiency:

It's the capacity to achieve your goal in the best way.

Effectiveness:

It's the capacity to achieve the expected effect.

CHAPTER 10

REFLEXIONS

Sales are today, not tomorrow. This must be our permanent thought.

Let us always remember: act with facts (sales) and results, not only words.

Let's be strong as an oak and flexible as bamboo. This means that we must be strong as an oak in our lives but flexible at the same time against difficulties and changes that arise. The popular saying «strong as an oak» means a person with great resistance, strength, and healthy.

The bamboo grows downward in the first seven years, spreading its roots to the depth. It's preparing to achieve its greatest success and become the fastest-growing plant in the plant kingdom. It isn't easy to barge in this world powerfully; you have to work hard for it.

An inspiring reading and a sales classic

The bestseller *The Greatest Salesman in the World* by Og Mandino, first published in 1968 and re-issued by Bantam Books.

Synopsis of the work

Hafid, unhappy with his life, approached his protector Pathros, a potentate merchant to whom he asks advice to become a powerful man like him and thus one day achieve the title of Greatest Salesman in the World. With this, Pathros is convinced that Hafid is the chosen one to be the new owner of 10 extraordinary scrolls that will teach him the arts of how to become the grandest salesman in the world.

The great teachings.

1. Form good habits and become their slave.
2. Greet each day with love.
3. I'll persist until I succeed.
4. I'm Nature's greatest miracle.
5. Live each day as it were my last.
6. Today, I'll be the master of my emotions.
7. I'll smile at the world.
8. Today, I'll multiply my value by a hundred percent.
9. I'll continue right now.
10. I'll pray for instructions and guidance.

Prayer, a fragment of the scroll number ten:

«Oh! Creator of all things, help me, for this day I go out into the world naked and alone, and without Your hand to guide me, I will wander far from the path which leads to success and happiness.

I ask not for gold or garments or even opportunities equal to my ability; instead, Lord, guide me so I may acquire skills similar to my opportunities.

You have taught the lion and the eagle how to hunt and prosper with teeth and claws. Teach me how to hunt with words and grow with love so I may be a lion among men and an eagle in the marketplace.

Help me remain humble through obstacles and failures, yet hide not the prize that will come with victory from my eyes.

Assign me tasks others have failed, yet guide me to pluck the seeds of success from their failures.

Confront me with fears that will temper my spirit, yet endow me with the courage to laugh at my misgivings.

Spare me enough days to reach my goals, yet help me live this day as though it is my last.

Guide me in my words that they may bear fruit, yet silence me from gossip that none be sullied.

Discipline me in the habit of trying and trying again, yet show me how to use the law of averages.

Favor me with alertness to recognize opportunity, yet endow me with patience which will concentrate my strength.

Bathe me in good habits that the bad ones may drown, yet grant me compassion for weakness in others. Suffer me to know that all things shall pass, yet help me to count my blessings today.

Expose me to hate so it not be a stranger, yet fill my cup with love to turn strangers into friends.

But all these things can be only if You will it. I am a small and lonely grape clutching the vine, yet though hast made me different from all others. Verily, there must be a special place for me.

Guide me, Lord, help me, Lord, show me the way, bless me with your Holy Spirit, dwell in my heart, and let me become all you planned for me when my seed was planted and selected by you to sprout in the vineyard of the world.

Help this humble salesman.
Guide me, God.
Amen»
Og Mandino (1977).

Let's pray, let us give thanks, thanks, thanks every day for our life, love, healthy body and mind, prosperity, and success.

Help this humble servant.

We have everything we need to succeed; we know the secret of selling, motivation, and the method to achieve it.

Dear **advisors** and **friends,** readers committed to your success, let's choose our venture, team, company, product, or service, and everybody can win.

Let's go… Always up!

I hope you benefit from this book. Thank you very much for such a lovely experience.

Juan Pablo Alviar Malabet
Jalviar518@gmail.com

ABOUT THE AUTHOR

Juan Pablo Alviar is a lawyer, salesman, entrepreneur, and businessman in different business branches with more than twenty-six years of commercial experience in various countries, passionate about the commercial subjects of law and new technologies.

With the desire to convey all his knowledge in the sales and motivation area, he decided to write his first book, The Secret of Selling and Motivation, in which he demonstrates that the secret works ideally under challenging times, in any country on this planet, which he has proven after his own two experiences lived in two different and extreme scenarios, such as the economic and oil strike in Venezuela and now during the COVID-19 pandemic in Colombia and Peru.

Among his achievements stand out being the founder of several programmed savings companies in different Latin American countries, in which he continues with the international expansion of this little-known and worldwide implemented activity. He has participated in the construction of customer portfolios with more than 85,000 people.

Currently, he is the director of several companies in different countries such as the United States, Colombia, Peru, and Venezuela, whose economic activities are developed in the areas of programmed savings, insurance, events, e-commerce, and technology.